"I have known Nicola & Luke Vardy for a good number of years, both as friends and associates ministers, and have on many occasions had the joy of hearing Nicola share her testimony to great effect in many of our missions around the U.K and overseas. Her story is one of redeeming grace, told with gutsy honesty and compassion for those carrying the same hurt and caught in the same circumstances that she was. Many identify with, and thus are touched and transformed by the grace of God in the same way as Nicola's life has been when they hear her story. I would heartily recommend Luke and Nicola's ministry "Ignite" to you, believing that their lives, testimony, and ministry will be as much of a blessing to you as it has been already to thousands around the world."

Jonathan Conrathe
Founder & Director,
Mission24

"Nicola's is a truly remarkable story of what happens when our worst brokenness, pain and horror collides with the grace and kindness of Jesus. He repairs, restores, redeems and revives us, with such gentleness and power we cannot resist His love. If you, or someone you know, simply cannot imagine how God could turn around your most painful experiences and make something outrageously powerful of them, then read this book! This is the Divine Gospel at work in the real world!"

Jarrod Cooper
Author, songwriter, broadcaster

UNBROKEN

A true story of a courageous
young woman's life

NICOLA VARDY

DEDICATION

I dedicate this book to my incredible husband.
I love everything we have been, everything we are
and all we are about to become.
Together jumping life's hardest obstacles. Hand in
hand starting new adventures, making memories of so
many precious, priceless moments along the way.
I love you!

CONTENTS

Introduction

My story begins when I was just a little girl. I was raised in a loving family and, in many ways, the centre of their world. My parents married young and had a happy marriage. Family outweighed ambition, but the determination of giving my brother and myself a good future gave them their focus to succeed.

My dad is an outstanding man. He is loving and gentle. My dad would often walk in through the front door, having done long hours at work, not even take off his coat and come straight out through the back door and into the garden to play with my brother and I. Mum is affectionate and full of love. In all her ways, she taught me life had no limitations. She taught me not to reach for the sky, but the stars beyond it.

I was close to my brother. We hung out together and often went on adventures. Being a little older, he looked out for me.

Confident, happy and determined, life was fun.

My parents taught me many things in life. Integrity and respect for others, as well as myself being the foundation. My dad taught me how to ride a bike. He held the back of the seat tightly and ran the whole way alongside of me. We would go up and down the street over and over. My confidence developed and all of a sudden, courage took over. I peddled so fast, in all the excitement, I hadn't noticed my dad had let go.   I smashed it. I was riding my bike. Well actually, it wasn't my own bike that my parents had bought me, but my brothers that I loved. Mine was purple, shiny and girly with a basket attached to the front. My brother's was red, old and battered by now, but much more respected amongst the boys I wanted to ride with.   I remember that moment, feeling like I had conquered the world, overcome life's hardest obstacle with my Dad praising my new found talent. This became my strength and became my ways through his teaching me to swim, to catch a ball, to run my fastest, to focus on the goal at hand, and to believe in myself. As a family, we had many holidays. Often, we would drive through the night to Scotland. In the early hours of the morning, we would set sale across the rough Irish Sea to Belfast. Mum was often sea sick on the boat, but my brother and I would run around enjoying every minute of it. Visiting my grandma and all our aunts and uncles are my fondest memories. I loved been a part of a big family and wished there wasn't an ocean separating us. I was spoiled and, to be honest, I was ok with that. Weekends away to the nicest of beaches, digging sand castles with my dad, and throwing the frisbee with my brother was always loads of fun. We spent many school summer holidays in London, staying with my mums friends in their huge house. It had its own swimming pool. My brother, my dad and I spent hours playing in that pool. Mum's friend Sue had two dogs: Callie Ann and Penny. I spent hours walking them around what seemed like a forest that wrapped around the garden. I loved dogs and always wanted one, but our cat, Pud, would not have been so keen. We always had days out. Theme parks, Alton Towers been my favourite. My mum, dad, my brother and I laughed so much as we got hit by the water and were left soaked by the rides.

Life was easy; I knew no struggle

There were always birthday party's filled with friends, party games and prizes. There were presents and loads of buns. An avalanche of gifts covered the whole lounge floor at Christmas. The house always smelled amazing when dad came home with the tree. The underfloor heating was on, and the house was filled with bright decorations. Christmas cards hung from every wall, and mum always made her own chocolate truffles and the most delicious ice cream.

I was dressed in expensive clothes and my hair was always styled, but I couldn't keep clean for long. Life was an adventure, and dirt seemed to find me. Trees were my thing. They took skill and courage to climb. Nobody dare go as high as me.

We lived in an area where families struggled financially. Many   lived in council accommodation and struggled to find work. I knew every person by name and often spent time in their homes. School was a positive part of my life. I had so many friends and often found favour with the teachers.

Mum was a Christian and took my brother and I to church. Dad respected her belief but took no part in it. Sunday school was difficult. I struggled to understand the teaching and was often asked to leave the room for not paying attention. Adults talked way beyond my understanding and took for what seemed like forever to tell a story. But, I had lots of friends there and enjoyed playing in the huge church garden after service. We ate sandwiches and home-baked cakes with nobody accounting for our portions of deserts. We played hide and seek in the many rooms of such a big old building.

My life was complete in every way.

One day, we had a church trip. I was so excited as the huge coach pulled up. We all piled on singing church songs throughout the long journey. We pulled up in a big car park and walked through the entrance doors to a huge football stadium. I was shocked by the volume of people worshipping God. It took my breath away. Wow, I thought to myself as I entered the mass seating area. My friends had never been to church and never been taught the stories I had heard in Sunday school. They had no understanding of God or who He was.

I thought our church was the only church. I had no idea others believed the same stories and knew our songs. An evangelist named Billy Graham went on to preach a message to the crowd of people. I had no clue what he said. I was too young to understand his story but many people, including my brother, responded to his invitation to come onto the field.

UNBROKEN

Quiet voice

Early one evening, at just nine years old, I was alone in my bedroom. Being the adventurous and imaginative character I was, my teddies and I were having fun. Church Songs were playing quietly in the background of the room, but as I played, the words in that soft distance started grabbing hold of me.

'Jesus take me as I am, I can come no other way.'

The words repeated over and over. Something *started happening in my heart.* Tears fell down my cheeks and a heat came over me. I was quiet and still, not afraid but feeling like I was wrapped up in a warm blanket and embraced. The heat was pouring out over every part of me. I wiped the tears back, and looked up to see *Jesus sitting beside me.* My heart was beating so fast, but my breathing I was trying to hold back.

Can you Imagine that moment

I sat still, staring in complete amazement. Daring not to blink or gulp in case it ended that moment. The man in the story all those years ago was sitting in my bedroom, amongst my teddies and looking only at me.

He was real, the stories were true

There was no Gospel to be heard, no preacher to take me through a prayer. I had no understanding of church, what to say or what to do.

"Jesus take me as I am,"
I asked softly in tears.

The tears just fell. I had everything in life, and somehow in those moments, it was like I had been missing the biggest part. Jesus was real, so the stories of heaven must be true I thought to myself. Life was forever, or at least it seemed it at that age, but now I knew we all could all go on to an even more amazing place. Surrounded in this incredible heat, *Jesus became my personal friend.* I ran downstairs as fast I could, missing a few steps, and told my mum I had just seen Jesus. She smiled and hugged me tight.

UNBROKEN

Gripped by fear

Early one morning, I set off to school. I walked down the street where I often played. At the end, there was a busy road. I crossed it every day and put no thought into it. Watching the cars go by, I was waiting to cross, when a blue lorry stopped, and the driver allowed me to cross. I waved, and thanked him on my way. I walked into the estate slowly in no rush and was trying to kick the smallest stones when I noticed that the blue lorry was moving slowly beside me. I looked up, smiling at the man who had helped me cross the road. He smiled and waved back. I continued kicking the stones, playing on my way. The man knocked on his lorry window catching my attention. He laughed as I celebrated the goal I had just scored with a really small stone. It was impressive, and I was happy with his applause.

My path continued, and my pace was slow. I found it odd after a while that the man was driving at my walking pace and continually smiling and waving at me. Soon, I felt a little uncomfortable as my own explanations started to arise.

I started to walk fast, but as I picked up pace so did the lorry. I was panicking inside but trying not to show it.

I was raised to be polite and respectful of everybody, and certainly anybody who had given me help. But somehow I knew being polite was no longer appropriate. The man knocked on his window and beeped his horn, but I no longer looked up. Keeping my head down, I walked as fast as my little legs could take me. *My hands were sweating. My legs were shaking.* I'd never experienced anything like this before. I was so scared. It didn't seem to matter what street I turned down. He was there. *It didn't matter how fast I walked or how long I'd ignored him. He was still there.*

I arrived at my school friend Julie's house. I quickly told Julie's mum, Hannah, all about the man. She laughed and then smiled at the man sitting in his lorry parked right outside her garden. Hannah put her arms around me laughing whilst telling me I had such a great imagination.

I took off my coat and ran upstairs to Julie, forgetting all about it. Sometime later, our coats went on, and Julie, and I were setting off to school. The door opened and, to my shock, the blue lorry was still parked outside Julie's garden. The man was looking straight at me, smiling. Looking at Hannah, *I was certain she would now believe* me that something was wrong. But she smiled and told me everything was ok, and explained that the man was probably delivering something to a neighbour.

We set off walking down the garden path. The man right at that moment started his engine. I looked back at Hannah as she was stood in the doorway about to wave us off. "Go on," she said. "Don't be late for school," she called, whilst waving us off. We walked down the long street, and I continued to look back at Hannah for reassurance as the man was driving at our walking pace. She continued to wave us on and I took reassurance this time I wasn't alone. We reached the end of Julies street, and the man beeped his horn. Arm-in-arm with Julie, I dared to look back. I saw him wave at me, he was laughing and then quickly drove off. My nightmare was over, and I burst out laughing with relief. I did have a great imagination, but I didn't like that ability that morning.

We skipped, laughed and talked, forgetting all about the man and his lorry. We had nearly reached the end of another street, when *all of a sudden I heard a voice telling me with an urgency to turn back. I* stopped and listened. "Nicola turn back, turn back." *What was that? Who was that? Why do I need to turn back?* I was startled   by the voice and confused by the instructions of it. The voice was real but impossible to explain. I heard the urgency of the words and, without hesitation, I stopped.   "Julie," I said abruptly, "we have to turn back".

She was laughing and continued walking. A large hedge was along the path blocking our view to our next steps. My chest felt like it had been tugged and pulled. The urgency of the words resounding in my head and *fear started to rise up inside of me.* Just a few steps later the corner now complete. We stood at the roadside waiting to cross. There stood a huge block of flats with a green area wrapped around it. On the edge of the grass was a little old bench with a man sitting reading his newspaper. My heart was beating so fast as I saw the man. "Julie," I said grabbing hold of her, "that's the man   from the blue lorry." Julie giggling and pulling away said, "how can you know that, you can only see his legs." "But it is," I replied. I could not explain it, but I   knew with complete certainty it was him.

I held onto her jacket desperately trying to pull her back, but she continued without me. I didn't want to be alone, so I ran the few steps and caught up with her. As our feet touched the path on the man's side of the road, I felt sick. My legs were shaking, and I was holding my breath as if sneaking past quietly he might not see us. I was trying to nudge Julie away from the inside of the path to give me space from him. As we walked quietly passed, Julie suddenly pushed me back, leaving me uncomfortably close to him.

I was looking at Julies face, as we passed the bench, looking for reassurance. But the moment her smile disappeared, and her face told the most unimaginable story, I was gripped by fear. Julie ran. *I was screaming so loud and running so fast.* I felt sick. My imagination was running even faster ahead of me, and I was imagining horrible things. As Julie got further and further away, the reality hit me. I was frozen. I was incapable of moving. My legs were shaking, and I had no control of them. I was holding my breath, but my heart was thumping out of my chest so loudly. He had to see that fear had gripped me.

The newspaper crunched   as he slowly lowered it. The old bench creaked   as he steadily lifted from it.

I was screaming at myself inside, "Run Nicola! Run!"

The footsteps got louder as he got closer. I could hear his deep breathing getting louder   as   he got closer.   It was as if time froze as he moved towards me but I couldn't react. That moment installed a fear within me that was inescapable.

UNBROKEN

Brave

I woke up laying on the grass. I think I must of passed out, but I have no idea in all honesty. I don't recall anything after his breathing got so close I could feel it on my neck. There were people all around me talking amongst themselves, and one telling me that I was safe now.

The police took Julie and me back to her house. We were questioned and told we were very brave and lucky girls.

Watching the news one day, I was shocked to come face-to-face with his face once again. I was tremendously disturbed to learn that the man had taken the lives of many little girls.

Life had changed in every way for me after that morning on my way to school. The bubble had burst. The world was dangerous. I now knew fear. It consumed me.

My brother and I had played pirate ships in the garden. The tall fence had been the ship walls itself. We punched little knots of wood out of each panel making spy holes to keep an eye on the baddies. But now it was as if the man was spying through the holes at me. The shed just at the bottom of our garden, where for hours I would play with Benjamin my rabbit who lived in there was no longer a place I could be. I felt unsafe. The streets where I played on my roller boots and my bike were no longer an option for me.

I was trapped by fear and constantly felt unsafe. I played at my mums feet and sang at the door when she took a bath. My bedroom now seemed scary. There were odd noises during the night, and shadows moving around behind the curtains. I would sneak into my brother's bedroom at night when everyone was asleep and slept on the floor beside his bed. My ordeal was over but the effects would last a lifetime.

The man was eventually   found and sentenced to prison. He was never to answer for the terror and torture he caused me that day. The uncountable fear I owned. The lack of trust in my own abilities to help myself in such a situation left me feeling vulnerable. I hated myself for not owning the strength to run.

He was given a life sentence. But my sentence had already began the moment he left the bench.

"No" became my comfort blanket to every invitation and opportunity. No longer enjoying school, I dreaded every day. Play time was the worst part of the day because my friends would play hide and seek. But as the police hadn't recovered my belongings that morning, I was sure, armed with my school books he would seek me out on the playground. He hadn't seemed bothered that morning that it was daylight, or that I was just moments away from my home. He seemed to have a confidence over Hannah and in the open space of the estate with the block of flats and all those windows it contained. Anybody could have been watching, but it didn't seem to bother him. He was a baddie and lived that way. I waited by the door for the school bell to ring and my torture to be over.

Shaped

My family relocated. My parents bought a house in an upright village that they really couldn't afford. But giving my brother and I a better and safer future, they committed to working even harder and longer. Starting a new school wasn't easy. I knew not one person. The school itself was never ending corridors and additional sections. *It was so big, and I felt so small.* I walked into the classroom and as the teacher announced my arrival, I saw all these faces staring back at me. It was obvious I was raised to still be the little girl I was, and my new classmates were way more grown up than I.

The girls befriended me and helped me settle in. They said I needed to dress better. My sensible footwear and crisp ironed shirt no longer fit in.

Rolling up my skirt and pulling down my socks was just the beginning. Smoking was the popular thing to do. The stench was horrible. I choked at every attempt, but with my friends encouragement and belief in me, I eventually I got the hang of it.

Shoplifting I became good at. My new friend introduced me to the way of it   and had my back the whole time. It was meant to be fun and exciting, but In truth it was terrifying.

I was being been shaped and moulded into my new surroundings.

Nicola was a baby's name. My friends renamed me Nikki. One evening at the park, a crowd of my friends and I were hanging out, when a guy approached us swearing and being assertive. I froze.

My hands were sweating and my legs shaking uncontrollably. I burst into tears with relief as he hugged my friends. He wasn't a stranger, just a friend with strange ways.

It became obvious to everyone, I was different. The more noticeable it became, the more the pressure increased for me to prove myself as normal.

My best friend confided in me that people were talking about me. She urged me to loosen up a little. I was a shy girl and aware of every noise around me. I never accepted anybody's kind gestures, especially anybody in a car allowing me to cross the road. I trusted nobody, and it was obvious.

Desperate to fit in, one evening my friend Sally gave me some alcohol. It stunk terribly and felt like it was burning my mouth as it went down. I held my nose tight as I forced myself to swallow it. My mouth felt numb like when the dentist gives you an injection. My head floppy and unable to walk straight amused me and set me off laughing. Once I started, I could not stop. No more constantly looking out for danger I found freedom, in being drunk. Wearing little black dresses, and becoming the fearless drunk party girl, I was every guy's trophy girlfriend and was popular for all the wrong reasons.

I'd become everything my parents raised me not to be.

Walking through the nightclub doors looking my best and, just hours later, falling out of them looking my worst. Wearing little tight dresses to mask an ocean of insecurities. Drunk and alone, the police found me laying in a gutter in the town centre. I was just 15 years old. Vomit all over my hair and mascara smudged all over my face, I was taken home.

My mum opened the door, tears running down her face whilst she helped the police officers hold me up under the shower. This wasn't the first time. The police often found me and got me home safe. My dad came in from work, disappointed at the state I was in. The police officer said softly but directly to me, "If we pick you up again, we won't be bringing you home; we will be taking you into care." *My dad looked helpless at my efforts to destroy myself.* Those words brought the reality of life that had been missing for too long. I loved my family. I didn't mean to hurt them. I was broken.

Nobody could fix me, and I knew it.

After leaving school, I got a job that I loved, working at a jewellers. I became really great friends with my work colleagues and thrived at my job. I worked every hour I could and thrived in such a short time there. I struggled with my education. Dyslexia made it impossible to keep up. I was a slow writer and the blackboard work would be regularly cleaned before I had the time to complete it. Big words were a stumbling block. I didn't understand sentences when they were thrown in, and spelling made my brain hurt, as I tried to figure out the letters needed to make the word, it often felt like I was tearing my mind apart trying to figure it out. I could hear the sound but not identify the letters needed. I failed at my education and left school with only friendships around me. This was my moment to shine. I was so intrigued by the diamonds. It was as though my brain kicked into gear with the interest I owned in them. I loved every aspect of my new role: taking stock counts and ordering supplies, learning fascinating facts about valuable stones and identification valuing. Away from my school friends, I was searching for myself, peeling back the layers others had shaped and moulded around me. No longer drinking, or shoplifting, I was gaining confidence in my new role.

I remember selling diamond rings to couples so in love, truly believing that I would never meet anybody who could ever win my heart or could love me as anything other than their trophy.

Trapped

Early one morning, I was walking my dog down the lane. I bumped into a guy I kinda of recognised from school. He knew who I was, and delighted to have the opportunity to approach me. He asked if he could accompany my walk. His manners amused me. We started talking, and something took me by surprise. I wasn't in a little black dress or wearing make up. In truth, I was wearing my dad's baggy jumper, and my hair was tied back. I wasn't drunk or scared. I was popular and, for some reason, he wasn't liked. But I didn't know why. He was different, a gentleman, as far as I could see. My words made him laugh, and I loved that he was enjoying the new me. Not the fake or fun girl I was expected to be. I was a sensitive girl, and it seemed he could see the vulnerable heart I'd hidden away. My face was beaming, it was hard to disguise. Together, we walked for ages. He invited me to hang out with him, but I was hesitant. I was *finally finding myself, but being able to be real with him was pulling me in.*

Soon, Alex and I were spending all our time together. I enjoyed hanging out with him and his family. Soon we were dating. Alex looked out for me. When I hadn't noticed guys were hitting on me, Alex would take them aside and defend me. They never seemed to bother me after they spoke. He made me feel safe and somehow protected. He took me to work and picked me up so that I didn't have to catch the bus. He was quite the gentleman, insisting on spending every break and lunch hour with me. My friends didn't like him, and stopped coming around. He told me how they flirted with him, so I was ok with them leaving because real friends didn't act that way. He bought me flowers and soft toys every payday. His parents could see that our relationship meant a lot to him, and they did their best to support it. Soon, we got engaged. It wasn't anything like every little girl's Prince Charming moment. I didn't love him. *But I thought being real was more valuable.*

My whole family was disappointed in the relationship. They couldn't understand what I saw in Alex. He had previously threatened to push passed my mum some time before when she had protected a younger boy in our house from him. But I knew it had been over me, and I felt protected in some strange way by his jealousy.

I thought he was misunderstood by my family and, as they didn't spend much time with him, I thought I knew him far better than they could.

The invitations sent, and the date fast approaching, my family constantly asking me to reconsider. My life was out of control, and I couldn't keep it from snowballing. I stopped eating in attempt to gain some kind of control. My mum was worried as the weight fell off. She would make me dinner every night, but as I came in late from work, I would hide in the kitchen feeding my dog my dinner. Throwing myself further into work, the time passed quickly, and I suddenly found myself standing in front of a mirror wearing a wedding dress that I knew in my heart I wasn't ready for.

The vows were exchanged as I gazed around, wishing with everything in me, I could run as far away as possible. Screaming inside but nobody could hear me. Gripped by the guilt of how his family had invested their time into me, I was unable to move.

Day became evening and I already felt trapped. Everyone was celebrating the day, but I felt so alone. I told my friend I had made the biggest mistake, and I needed her help to get out of it. She hugged me tight, calling me a dumpling, she said it was too late. I had been given every opportunity to agree with my family in the many months and ways they tried to get through to me that this relationship was wrong for me.

But it was only now I could see it.

I was devastated.

Two months into the marriage I was trying to make a good life for us both. Keeping the house spotless and cooking all the meals. I was no longer working in the jewellers. Alex couldn't stand the attention I was getting from customers. He had watched me in the doorway whilst I worked and pulled me up if it seemed like I was acting inappropriately.

Two years into the marriage, I sat staring at the doctor as he told me I was pregnant. I was the happiest girl in the whole world. I was too excited to restrain myself waiting for the bus home so I ran to my parents' house. Bursting through the door, I told them my news. They were so happy; the excitement filled the house. Alex reacted somewhat different. He said he was happy, but it was difficult by his response to believe. Soon, I had become a mummy in every way. No more tight dresses. No more late nights out.

Chemical-free cleaning and homemade food became my thing. I was no longer his trophy bride, and he began to resent me for it. I couldn't understand his need to smoke and drink, have late nights and act as if nothing had changed. Watching him get drunk and become argumentative, being rude to my mum and staying up all night, I'd lost all respect for Alex. He wasn't a gentleman, but a disgrace. He was no longer fun, but an embarrassment.

One evening, we had an argument. This was rare and over something insignificant. But, as I argued my case, he suddenly grabbed me really tight, shaking me and shouting at me. He threw me against the wall, pushing and pulling me to the floor and kicking me hard. I was terrified. He opened the front door and dragged me out onto the street.

A neighbour jumped out of her car and helped me up off the ground. She took me into her house and made me a hot drink. I was so embarrassed and ashamed.

The neighbour went to calm Alex down and later I returned home.

I was shocked and replaying the events over and over in my head. Eventually he fell to the floor and started to cry. "I'm sorry" he said. "You didn't deserve that, You deserve better than me." I put my arms around him and told him it was ok. It was far from ok, but this had never happened before or anything close to it. I blamed myself for pushing at him with words, giving him no space to think had pushed him into a reaction that he now was ashamed of.

Alex was a polite and gentle person mostly. I told myself that this was a one-off incident and worked harder at giving him space in future discussions.

Christopher was born and became my whole world. So perfect and so tiny.   I was scared to take my precious tiny baby home as Alex's outbursts had became regular and unpredictable. The arguments were unavoidable, even when I gave in he forced the situation to continue. I never knew what I would say or do next to upset him and cause his behaviour to change. I was made responsible for every thing anyone said to him. I had to side with his reasoning which was founded on paranoia and accept he was a victim of people's cruel views of him. I found myself lying constantly to my parents to protect his reputation and already fragile relationship with them. The day we left hospital I told my parents I had no idea how to look after a baby and asked if we could move in with them until I felt confident looking after Christopher alone. I often made out that I was incapable or accidental to cover up for Alex.

With no more arguments between us, a month later, we moved back home. Everything was great and a new chapter in our lives began. Christopher somehow brought us together, and I was finally happy.

Chloe was born just two years later, A girl they announced handing the most beautiful little bundle to me. I was so happy, and my heart was full. Family life had become natural to us both. We were still very young and money was a little tight, but we made the most of what we had and always put the children first.

Outgrowing our home we moved house. It was a thousand times nicer and bigger. Our new house was over an hour away. This was our fresh start, no more constant reminders or memories of earlier bad times. I was proud of the house and where we were living. A little farming village tucked away in the countryside. I soon made friends in the street, and the children loved their new school. Christopher was a shy boy, and Chloe was the total opposite. They soon had loads of friends and enjoyed their new beginnings.

Alex was working long hours and often working on days off. Tired, he became difficult to be around. He seemed to bring an atmosphere in with him. The children would become quiet and withdrawn when he was home. There was a tension, and I constantly felt like I was walking on an earthquake about to rumble. The house was spotless and the dinners were made. The children were bathed and the dog was walked, but no matter how much I cleaned and thought and planned ahead, he made me feel like a failure. I stopped going to my friends` house for coffees. I felt guilty for not being in the house. Even though the children were at school, and the house was spotless, somehow I felt unsettled socialising whilst he was at work.

The arguments started and the abuse began. He was so angry, but I had no clue why. He started to drink more and more. The lies were obvious and the abuse was relentless. I was losing all sense of normalcy and anything that was remotely acceptable.

I wore his old worn out clothes, and rarely bought anything for myself. He was the one working and needed to look his best whilst I was tucked away in the house alone cleaning.

Desperate

One morning, after the worst night of abuse before I took the children to school, my heart was bursting with pain. I had to encourage myself that I would make it home. *"Just one more step Nikki you can do this, just one more."*

Stepping through the door, I closed it slowly behind me. *I was broken in every way and the pain was suffocating.* Locking the door behind me, I slid down it. Hitting the floor in tears, I gazed across the room staring at the telephone.

I could ring my mum , but what words would I start with.

Religion did not save me

Jesus did

- Nicola Vardy

Life had been fake for so long;
every bruise had its own story.

I could ring my brother, but how will he be able to have a friendship with Alex after it. I could ring my friends, but their sympathy wouldn't change anything. I was so overwhelmed and aching so deep inside by the pain.

I laid on the floor holding myself as this loud harrowing noise came out of me. It was so big and uncontrollable. It was like something was reaching within me and dragging out the pain. The noise sounded desperate, and I could not hold onto it. With no ability to think, I laid in all my tears and the reality of the life I owned. Alone and burdened with such weight.

I heard a name I hadn't heard in a long time, loudly and desperately come out of my mouth.

Jesus heal me Restore me

Make me whole

In that instant, I felt a wave of heat embrace me, wrapping every part of me up. I saw a picture, like a photo, appear immediately in front of me. It was clear and in colour. My son, my daughter, myself and a tall man holding onto the handle of a pram. I didn't know the man, and didn't understand the contents of the picture, but I sobbed as I knew that Jesus was with me.

I could not believe that after all these years of ignoring Him, I called on His Name just once and He answered. I didn't beg or plead. In all my mess, in all my choices, just as I am, he answered. I was blown away that Jesus could give you pictures. Excited by the whole encounter and experience, I rang my mum. "Mum did you know that God can give you pictures like a photo?" "Yes," she replied. I told her all about the picture. She didn't know the situation and didn't understand the contents of the picture, but I felt her excitement as she thanked God I was reaching out to Him.

With so much excitement and   bursting with happiness, I had no idea how God could even start to fix my problem, but I knew I was no longer alone in it.   I cleaned the house singing the songs that I remembered from church,   and for the first time in what seemed like forever, I had Hope in my situation.

That evening, as Alex arrived home, he was really annoyed that I'd not picked up milk on my way home home from school.   I heard a voice, just like years before, on the morning I walked to school. The voice told me to pick up Alex's phone. Now I knew the voice was God. I was too afraid to pick up the phone because Alex had always made it clear that I was not to touch it. It was expensive, and I was clumsy according to Alex. Again I heard Gods voice. " pick up the phone". I was thinking of how I could sneak off with the phone just for a moment when Alex left to pick up some milk. Slamming the door behind him, this was my opportunity. I picked up the phone and read a message that lit up the screen. It was obvious Alex was having an affair with a work colleague. I called the number to discover the relationship had been going on for 18 months. I felt betrayed, but this was my opportunity to get out and I was taking it with both hands.

That night the marriage ended. Alex wasn't happy at my discovery and like many times before, fell to his knees crying for forgiveness for his mistakes. But I was strong and focused. Getting out was in my grasp and there was no way I would trap myself again. My dad walked into the reality of my life. The police were called. The locks were changed and after 9 years of marriage I stood in front of the doctor as he noted and recorded every bruise on my body.

I was so ashamed

"Nicola"

One evening, my mum invited me to church. I couldn't believe she could even consider it. I was ashamed of the bruises I wore and the divorce I was pursuing. Church wasn't for broken people but those righteous and all together.

"Nikki" she said, "you should have come to church. We had a brilliant meeting. There was a really nice guy there. I gave him a prophetic word and wrote it in his bible. I sat behind him all night asking God for you to meet and marry someone just like him." "Mum," I replied, "no way will I ever marry again."

Six months went by, and my mum again invited me to a women-only church meeting. "No mum," I

I gave God my mess

He turned it into a message

- Nicola Vardy

answered. "I don't know the language. I don't know the bible. I don't dress like a Christian or speak like a Christian. Church isn't for me. I don't fit in, and I can't do fake any longer."

Mum later came home from church. "Nikki," she said, "I met this lovely lady today. She invited me back to her house for a cup of tea before my long journey home. I was telling her all about your situation, and she encouraged me with her own story. You see, her son had been raised in church, but like you, he fell into the ways of the world. He became everything he wasn't, trying to prove himself in gangs. But God called him out of a nightclub and invaded his heart. Her son is now passionately perusing God in all His ways."

Mum was encouraged and, in all her excitement, was praying on the way home, "Oh Lord, could Nikki meet and marry someone just like her son?"

Been a single parent terrified me. All the statistics against my two beautiful, incredible, loving children ever succeeding in life were against them. The stigma of being from a broken home labelled them. Living on income support and being unable to provide anything other than a home was every reason I had stayed with Alex for so long.

"Nicola" God spoke. It felt strange. I hadn't been called or known myself as that name for so long. But as God continued to speak, I knew it was time to find the little girl I was-full of courage and adventurous ways. It was time to let God shape and mould me ,not my past.

Eighteen months had past. I was divorced and enjoying life. I was changing my ways, and enjoying my children in every part of it. The house became a home and the peace within it was appreciated.

My parents and friends were a huge support. My life truly was happy.

God would often speak to me. He would give a name with a number along with it. I had no idea what this meant, so I would ring my mum to discover it was a scripture in the Bible. Those scriptures were always a huge encouragement in everything I was facing during those times. I was hearing many things about the nations and the things that were to come, but I didn't understand why God would tell me these things. I had no voice and was in no position to warn our nations' leaders. So I just prayed into these things.

As I walked into the supermarkets, walked my dog through the fields, or sat in a coffee shop with friends, I would start having a knowledge of the situations of stranger's around me. It was very weird. I would pray, "Lord, heal that ladies leg. She's suffering with arthritis. Lord, send that man the money he needs for this month's bills. He's short because his washing machine broke. Lord, give that girl back her worth. She's giving herself so cheaply. Lord, give her back her identity."

God would speak to me all the time about others but rarely the details about myself.

It's time

Sitting quietly one Saturday afternoon, I was at my parents` house, when God spoke to me in a soft voice. "Nicola, I'm calling you to church." Immediately I panicked and answered, "Lord, I don't do happy clappy club, it's not for me." I started to busy myself, but again the Lord spoke, "Nicola, I'm calling you to church." I was panicking, my hands sweating at His suggestion and soon I replied, "Lord no, I can't. Don't ask me to go to a happy clappy club. It's not for me."

At that moment, my mum and her friend walked through the door. "Nicola," my mum said, "We were out praying over the fields for Israel, but God stopped me and said it was time for you to go to church."

Really? Really God? You brought my mum into this?"
I thought.

Leaving the room, I was trying to get away from
God. But His voice followed me. I found myself
sitting in the restroom pleading with God not to make
me go to church. Church to me was a happy clappy
club. People who were all together, happy and clappy
at church songs. They knew the Bible and had such
detailed accounts of the life JESUS lived. They spoke
in terms I couldn't understand, and a language that
was well, weird. They had perfect families and could
bake amazing cakes.

My life was far from theirs. I had nothing to give,
nothing for them to be encouraged by or gained from.
I was living on income support, and barley surviving
the cost of school uniforms and the Christmas season.
How could I give into the collection that landed on
your lap for all to see when I was already constantly
depending on my parents for financial help? I couldn't

teach them anything other than how to make mistakes and bad choices. I was unworthy for Jesus to hang on a tree and give His last breath for. I couldn't help myself, let alone help others. I just didn't have it in me to put on a brave face and fake it to survive once again.

Then, as I sat with fear building inside of me, that God really wanted me to do this, a sadness came over me. Remembering just a year or so before when I was sitting in all my mess, in an ocean of tears, carrying an uncountable pain, I called on His name just once, and He immediately answered. I hadn't begged or pleaded yet in that moment He came. I felt sick. God had now asked me several times and had asked through my mum, yet I was contending Him. Bravely, taking a deep breath I answered, "whatever you need me to go to church for,

You have one night,
and one night only to do it in."

Michelle, my mums friend, was delighted at my willingness and arranged to take me that very evening before I could change my mind. What sort of church opens on a Saturday and on an evening I thought. We got into the car and started the long journey to a church she felt God had put on her heart. Miles down the road, we were lost. We couldn't find the village and was starting to give up hope of ever finding it. A shopping centre was along the side of the road and Michelle suggested we stopped off for coffee before returning home. I was so, so happy. Excitedly, I agreed and was thanking God for not making me go through with this. I thought just maybe He was testing my willingness, but understood that the cost to me was just too great. As the indicators went on, I heard the voice of a God so gently again say again "Nicola, I'm calling you to church" . My smile sank as I told Michelle we had to go to church.

We were lost and miles away from home. With no clue which way to head, we got off the road. Pulling up, there was a gent just getting into his car. Michelle asked, "Sir, do you know where Wath Upon Dearne is?" He laughed and said, "actually I do. As it happens, I've just had a call from my daughter, and I'm on my way to her now. You may follow me if you like. She lives in Wath Upon Dearne." "Wow!," we said, "thank you." We followed the gent for half an hour and he eventually stopped and shouted to us, "this is Wath Upon Dearne."

With the window down, Michelle asked a couple walking their dog as they   passed by if they knew of a lively church in the area. She didn't know it's name, just the village it was near. The couple looked at each other laughing, "we don't go to church ourselves, but we have just passed a building up the road. We were discussing how noisy it was and we were thinking it was a church based on the songs."

On their directions, we headed up the road. Pulling up in the car park, it was packed. I felt so uncomfortable knowing we were   late and that many people would look at us, appalled at our late arrival.

I walked through the door behind Michelle. I was shocked at all I could see. I was terrified and holding onto the door handle as if somehow it was saving me.

People were shouting, laughing, screaming, dancing, singing, shaking and rolling around on the floor. It didn't look anything like a church, but every bit an accident scene.

A man holding a microphone came charging towards me. He was breathing loudly and stretching his arms out to people in his way. They fell down to the floor as his hands touched their heads. He never even looked back to them, he was looking only at me.

"Young lady" he said, "just before you walked through the door, God gave me a picture of you. He told me that you had been wronged by a man when you were a little girl, and you have been impregnated with fear ever since." As his words came out, I was weeping. This man knows my Jesus. He knows my friend who talks to me. He asked me if he could pray for me, I was terrified and said, "only if you use your words and not your hands." He looked at me startled. I said, "look what you have done to these people." We looked around the room together. There were bodies filling every area of the the floor. Some shaking and some rolling around. He said "ok close your eyes." But I stood back. "Only if you put your hands in your pockets," I replied. He looked very confused, "I won't close my eyes until I know your hands aren't free" I made my position clear. He tucked his hands in his pockets and declared the words, "fear be gone!"

I woke up some time later on the floor at the other side of the church. I can only imagine how I got there. Crawling off the floor, I saw a guy who was laughing from his belly. He looked like a baboon. I was embarrassed on his behalf. I said, "Lord, you can do anything to me tonight, but don't do that."

The people were all seated, and I was taken to the only seat in the building that was left. It was right behind the man with the microphone. Some time passed, and the laughing baboon dragged himself off the floor. Nathan, the man with the microphone, helped him up whilst laughing at him. The laughing baboon turned around and looked at me. I was stunned. I knew that face. I'd seen it a few years before on a picture that God had given me whilst I was sitting in all my brokenness and had called on His name. It felt like my mouth had hit the floor and had taken forever to simply smile. He said, "Hi, I'm Luke." I was thinking to myself … a laughing baboon, Lord? Really? "Hi, I'm Nicola," somehow followed.

Nathan got up and shared a story. I understood every word and felt encouraged by his passion and his belief he had in it. He said to the people with a confidence, "if you need anything from God, now is your moment." I didn't give myself time to think. I leaped out of my seat and ran to his feet. He laughed with surprise at my willingness for prayer. Oddly, I wasn't afraid. He asked, "What do you need from Jesus?" My reply stunned him. "Everything," I replied.

"Everything he has for me." I explained, "I've given God one night only for all he has for me in church." He smiled and said "I love that." "You asked for it," he said. I woke up in the driveway of my parents house. Apparently I was carried to the car hours after that prayer.

In the morning I felt like the world had been conquered, and I felt free. I asked Michelle to take me back to that church and that evening service. Again, I ran out for prayer. Tuesday pray evenings, Thursday study meetings, Saturday revival nights, Sunday morning and evening services, I was there.

Something amazing was happening. I was becoming me again. I had spent decades trying to fix myself and finally I was somehow being fixed. There seemed to be no particular moment, but I was being put back together in every way.

I don't know what message changed me or what prayer was answered, but as I sat with my friends at home and they laughed and spoke of others, I looked at them with a deep deep sadness. Did I really used to laugh with you about such things? Are this the conversations we had to fill our day? I sat hurting inside that I was ever that person. In that moment, I realised that when I gave my heart to Jesus, He had changed it.

God set me up

Six months of travelling and a lifetime of healing later, I invited my mum to join me for the first time at church. It had become my home and the people my family.

We sat there waiting for the service to start when my mum blurted out to me. "Over there, Nicola! That young man I know him." Pointing at Luke, she recalled writing a prophecy in the back of his Bible. I called Luke over and introduced him to my mum. 'I know you he said, I met you some time ago. We were visiting your church, and you sat behind me all night". My mum smiling recalled that evening. It was the night she invited me to church when I was bruised and ashamed of all I'd become. She recalled praying and asking God for me to meet and marry someone like him. She was laughing as I told her Luke was the guy in the picture I told her about years before.

Later that evening Luke asked my mum if she would come to his house and support the moment I would meet his parents. We had become good friends and often hung out together. We pulled up on the driveway, and Luke's mum opened the door. "Hello Dorothy," she said . "What? How does your mum know my mums name?" I asked Luke. "Hello Colleen," my mum replied as they embraced with a cuddle. Luke & I looked at each other totally confused. "Dorothy came to a women's meeting some time ago," Colleen went onto explain. "She had a long journey home, so I invited her back for a cup of tea." My mum looked at Luke smiling, "I heard all about how God had called you out of a nightclub and invaded your heart." She smiled recalling her prayer to God on her way home all that time ago. "Oh Lord, could Nikki meet and marry someone just like her son?"

Luke's family embraced me

On the very day of the first anniversary of me walking into church, Luke and I went on our first date. We had become really good friends, and in many ways, close. I'd never told Luke about the picture God had given me. If I were to ever give my heart to a guy, he would have to fight for it.

We went to a church where a   Gospel choir was singing the house down. We spent that evening under the anointing,   under the church seats. As we left to find a restaurant, our friends not realising we were on a date, decided to join us.

I could never have imagined how this evening would
become one of the best nights of my life.

As we chatted and laughed with our friends around the table. A couple behind us grabbed the attention of Luke and I. They asked what drugs we had taken and were confused when we said we didn't take drugs.

"What have you been drinking?" they asked. Again, they were confused as we told them we didn't drink. "Then why are you laughing?" they said. I was sad by their confusion. It reminded me all too quickly of the girl I used to be. My chains had been broken, my confidence restored. I was free in every way, but as I looked at their desperate faces, my heart broke into pieces. I had given Jesus my heart. He didn't just heal it, restore it and make it whole. He had changed it. And now I could see He was using it. Luke and I spent that evening telling this precious couple all about Jesus. We took them to church the next day and sat in tears together as they responded to the Gospel giving their hearts to Jesus.

As they left that service looking remarkably different to how they had arrived, they took our hands and said, "Many people wouldn't have looked at us, or taken the time out to speak with us. We're addicts and, to most people, a waste of space. But you guys gave us what you had, and we are changed for it".

Words that will forever remain in my heart.

Luke and I were soon inseparable. I adored him, and it was obvious. He made me laugh, and I literally could not hinder my smile. We hung out at the cinemas, went to restaurants and walked around lakes. I felt complete when I was with him. Luke is tall, blonde and blue-eyed. He was gentle and kind, a gentleman but with no hidden agenda. We spent hours talking and hours praying together. Now I knew what it was to be in love.

Luke bought me the biggest and most beautiful diamond ring. Placing it on my finger, he was shaking, which made us both laugh. The words he spoke I will forever treasure. Our families and friends were so happy. Christopher and Chloe jumped into our arms when they saw the ring. Luke had asked the children and my dad if he could marry me days before and was delighted in the way they embraced him. The children loved him, as did my mum. Well, she had prayed enough for him to marry me. Luke and I married three months later in 2006. It was a Christmas wedding and the most beautiful day. Our family and friends were so happy. My children became ours, as Luke became a father to them. Christopher was ten years old and Chloe eight years old. As we signed the marriage documents, Christopher in the excitement asked my dad what we were doing. He answered, "Christopher, Luke is signing the papers to say he will love your mummy for the rest of his life." Christopher was so happy, he was in tears.

Destiny

Today, I wear the most beautiful diamond ring, given by a guy who not only calls me precious, and continually treats me with honour, but who loves me wholeheartedly.

I'm not his trophy, but his best friend. Luke led me to Jesus before himself. In all his ways, he enabled my relationship with Jesus to become even stronger. He has taught me the ways of God, and helped me study the Word along the way.

He continues to gives the very best of himself to me.

Satan tried to destroy me but

my God restored me

- Nicola Vardy

I love Luke with all of my heart . He's my rock, my hero and my best friend.

So today we celebrate 13 Incredible, Amazing Happy years of marriage. It's been a journey that has made us laugh, made us strong and brought out the best of each other. We jumped life's hardest obstacles together, cried   together and believed God together. We have held each other up when others have hurt us and pushed each other to achieve our goals. We've pursued the Fire and watched each other go after God In   all His ways.

I Love doing life with this crazy, fun, amazing guy. His relentless reach for souls and His passion for the Kingdom of God   inspires me to continually push myself. Luke believes in me when I struggle to believe in myself. He encourages the best to come out of me and continually seeks the gold God has put into me. My no's became my let's do this.

His love and His ways with me

continually astound me.

Christopher and Chloe smashed their exams and got degrees. They're incredible kids, and I could not be happier for all they themselves have achieved, the hearts they own, and the futures they pursue. They're outstanding individuals and a pleasure to everyone who meets them.

Baptised together, doing missions in children's orphanages in Latvia together, going to the nations themselves, preaching the Gospel and pastoring the youth together. They are best friends and look out for each other.

Christopher now married with a child of his own, he ripped down every statement of a boy from a broken home. It's not what he remembers or what defines him today, but his achievements and hard work that he himself embraced along the way. The love he was raised in and the home together Luke and I gave him, is how he remembers his childhood today.

Chloe is about to step into her next chapter, leaving Bible college this summer. She has so much to give from all she has faced and conquered, and such a drive and ambition that will show the world how to shine. She's funny, and makes us laugh, quirky with a unique oddness that continues to amuse us. She's adventures and fearless, confident and determined.

Our family expanded with the arrival of Atlanta, She's the funniest, quirkiest, intelligent little girl. She loves cuddles and drawing. Quite the masterpiece when it comes to animals. Her passion is singing and writing her own songs. Our home often Reaps her talents.

Isiah came and completed our family. He's such a loving boy and has the biggest of hearts for the homeless people. He cries at the reality of their lives and can't understand why they don't have a home. Isiah loves his Bible and often we find him praying in his room . His talents are obvious as he builds the most detailed incredible scenes with his Legos. He loves playing on his console and riding his bike. Our children are our world.

I love everything we are
and all we are about to become

Prison

Looking back at the very first day I ever went into prison to support my Pastor and his team in the wonderful ways they were sharing Jesus with so many prisoners truly has had an impact on my life today.

My Pastor, Peter Morris, had asked me many times to go in and share my story, to only ever hear the words "I can't do that" but one time was different. I reflected over all the many hours that Peter had sat with me in those first few months of going to church as I cried through all my pain and talked through all my battles.

He gave me the very best of himself and I in my heart wanted to give something back.

I don't know your story

but mine got better

when Jesus stepped in

- Nicola Vardy

The prisoners were somebody's to him. they were a part of his heart and his mission field. I didn't get it, to me they were everyone I feared. The one I held my breath at when I hear a noise through the night. The one I ever dread looking at wrongly in the street. The one who's the reason my children play under lock and key. To know the doors would   shut with an echo behind me and keys would constantly rattle around me gave my resistance ground.

I found myself out of gratitude for Peter's support, handing over my belongings and trying to gulp quietly at the first door of a very big prison. I was shocked to find a room with 30 or so guys from all different cultures and backgrounds so friendly and welcoming, polite and so real. I went on to share my story many times over the years and never at any time did I ever see one guy look remotely comfortable.

Whilst with total respect they listened intently to me reliving the time that the stranger changed my world. The prisoners would cry and couldn't hide it, they tried because weakness for them could have caused them problems. They would shake under the presence of God. This confused others but not one prisoner ever asked to leave the room. They were allowed to ask questions and every time it was the same one

"How are you so together"

I remember being asked on my first visit whilst I was sat beside Peter, if I had forgiven the man, who I'd described as a monster throughout my story and Alex, the man I should have been able to trust. I looked at Peter knowing what the right answer should have been, representing a Christian ministry of course my answer should have been effortless to answer, but I had to tell the truth and my answer of course was no. I just couldn't forgive either of them for the pain they had caused me.

But sitting in the same seat just two years later, I was again confronted with that same question.

"Have you forgiven the man and Alex" he asked "yes"
I confirmed confidentiality. And honestly. Wow, I
thought when did that happen.

Many of the prisoners shared their own stories with
me. I came to realise that not one of their actions
came out of wholeness but out of the brokenness of
their own journeys.

My heart was changed, and my chains were broken.
No longer did I need to live a life of pain, but I was
free of now hating a complete stranger who wronged
me decades before. Who could have ever imagined
that God would use me in the very thing that broke me.

I've seen those prisoners become evangelists, pastors,
preachers and vicars. Completely transformed by the
Gospel and the love of the team.

One man Luke and I loved with all our hearts, was one of our best friends and my solid support through my firsts months of coming to church was once a prisoner. He watched over my home whilst I lived there miles away from my family, alone with my young children in the months leading up to Luke & I getting married.

He and my dad decorated my house and for hours he worshipped in tongues, my dad had no clue what he was singing but felt the peace fill the house.

I'm so glad I confronted my fears, I overcame them and *broke out of my own prison cell.*

Ministry

Life with Jesus continues to amaze me. His ways are so limitless and His plans are huge. Luke and I have traveled the world preaching the Gospel of Jesus Christ. We have seen *thousands respond to the Gospel* and *countless miracles* that have *undone our hearts* many times.

I will forever hold dear the time I met Rose. A beautiful elderly lady who was so graceful and gentle was passing by. Luke and I were working alongside a church in their summer outreach. Rose was on her way home passing by the park where we had many activities set up to reach the community. Rose and I somehow bumped into one another, and chatted pleasantly.

I noticed after a while that Rose was uncomfortable and seemingly suffering with some pain. I asked Rose if she had a problem. She went on to tell me that she had recently fallen down some concrete stairs whilst on holiday abroad. She had broken her ankle and was still recovering the surgery.

I was surprised to hear of her trauma. I asked if I could have a look, she pulled up her trouser leg a little. I was quite shocked to see her ankle so heavily bruised and massively swollen. "Rose" I said " this must be causing you so much pain, can I pray for you" she smiled softly " oh I don't believe in God" she answered. " but I do" I replied with an even bigger smile than her own. She went on to agree that if I didn't mind looking silly praying for her than she would be willing to allow me to do so.

I knelt down in the grass, wrapping my hands around her very sore ankle and prayed "In the Name of Jesus be healed" suddenly I felt my hands were loose around her ankle, opening my eyes to see the swelling had completely gone. In that moment I wanted to shout as loud as possible *"That's my Jesus"* but wisdom took over as I slowly stood up. " thank you for allowing me to pray for you Rose" I said holding back the excitement I contained. We continued to talk and as it was time for her to leave I said "Rose, I've noticed you don't seem to be as uncomfortable as you were whilst we've been talking, does your ankle feel any different". Looking slightly puzzled she moved her foot around. "Oh" she said. "It feels quite different" smiling I said " if it feels different, maybe it looks different, should we have a look" knowing it did I thought it was time for her to come face to face with her miracle.

Lifting up her trouser leg again slowly, her entire face lit up as did mine. Not only had the swelling completely disappeared but so had every trace of the bruising. Holding my hands in her own she gazing at me with tears dropping down her cheeks said "oh dear, *He's real isn't He*. All these years I thought church was nothing more than a nice gesture, never did I know that *He is real"*. We smiled, embraced one another and I had the privilege to lead Rose to Jesus.

Blind eyes open, deaf ears open, spines realigning, lumps disappearing, PARALYSED legs working, brand new teeth appearing to name a few.

We have seen God work in so many amazing ways so many stories but that is a another book.

We have had the privilege to travel with the Founder and Evangilist Jonathan Conrathe of Mission 24 Ministries. Traveling through Europe and overseas together. He has nurtured our gifting and developed our skills. He has Invested hours of himself into us, whilst loving us and believing in us. Today Luke is and associate Evangelist of Mission 24 Ministries.

That moment when Jesus becomes real to that precious individual is the very reason that today we work tirelessly to reach the world to further the kingdom of Jesus Christ.

Luke and I launched Ignite Ministries and in October 2019 we took the further and deeper step giving up our entire family income to live by faith and step into the fullness of our calling to the Nations.

If you would like a personal relationship with Jesus pray this prayer:

Jesus,

I don't know you yet, but I understand that you know me. I have heard stories of you changing people's lives and turning around hopeless situations. So far I have not lived my best life, but I now know that this is not the end for me. I choose to believe that you know the way out for me, and that with your help you can take me there. I thank you that you waited for me, and even now you offer me help. So Jesus, help me. Guide my life and help me fulfil my potential. I choose to trust you with my whole life, and as I do I pray that you will help me to understand and know you more. I want you to be my friend, my Father, my counsellor, my hope, my joy and my strength… Amen

UNBROKEN

If you would like to connect with Ignite our ministry and support us in taking the Gospel to the precious people of the nations please visit our website:

www.igniteministries.co.uk

We wholeheartedly value and appreciate your support in sending us.

UNBROKEN

Go into all the world

IgniteMinistries

UNBROKEN

UNBROKEN

UNBROKEN

Printed in Poland
by Amazon Fulfillment
Poland Sp. z o.o., Wrocław